Penelope,

Many people around the world
use sign language.
Did you know that each country
has their own kind?
Mikah uses Australian sign
(Auslan)
I hope you notice how different
it is from the signs you know ☺
Enjoy the book

With love
from
Mikah and Tabitha

2019.

Mikah's Big Move
First published in Australia in 2018

Written by Tabitha Jean Page
Illustrated by Alexander Kulieshov

Ilustrator details
Email- beMAAA@yahoo.com

Book Title – Mikah's Big Move
Series name- Mikah can!
Book number in series- One
ISBN –978 0 6482704 0 9

Publisher/Author details
Web- https://www.tabithajeanpage.com/
Email- tpagewriter@gmail.com

Proofread by Monika Konksi

Edited by Sally Odgers
http://www.affordablemanuscriptassessments.com/

Printed and bound by IngramSpark
ingramsparkaustralia@ingramcontent.com
ingramsparkinternational@ingramcontent.com

written by
TABITHA J PAGE

Mikah's Big Move

Illustrated by
ALEXANDER KULIESHOV

To my little monkeys, I love you.
X x Tab

To my wifey who always supports me.
Alex

Mikah monkey lives at the zoo with his
family.
Every day is the same.

He wakes up...
He eats breakfast...
He stretches...

Then the zoo opens and it's time to play.

Mikah dances and struts around like a happy peacock, showing off for visitors.

Children squish their faces into the fence.
Mikah copies them which always makes people giggle.

The visitors are his friends.

When the zoo gates close at night Mikah is tired from his antics, but he still has important things to do.

Mikah was born deaf, so keeper Annie teaches him how to talk with his hands.
Every day Mikah and his family practise sign language before bedtime.
If he practises enough, Mikah will soon be a pro.

Mikah loves his home and his routine.
Nothing ever changes.
That makes him feel calm and safe.

One afternoon a sign is put on the fence
-Moving to new enclosure-

Visitors read it aloud.
Big sister Maizi signs to tell Mikah what it means.

'No!' Mikah grumps.
'I won't go!'

'Why not?' Mum asks.

'I like our home and my friends know I'm here.'

'You can still do the same things in our new house.
You'll be fine, trust me.'

Mikah is not convinced. He stages a sit-in. No one is taking him anywhere!
Moving day comes and high in a tree perches Mikah monkey.

'Mikah, come down,' keeper Annie signs.

'No.' Mikah pouts.

'Please,' Dad gestures.

'No.'

Keeper Annie cannot climb high enough to reach him.
Mum is hopping mad.
'Mikah monkey, get down here!'

Mikah blows raspberries.

Keeper Annie takes Maizi and Dad to their new home.
Mum strolls towards the gate, ready to leave as well.

Wait... 'No!'

Mikah scrambles down the tree.

Mikah frowns.
'It's scary… I don't want to go.'

'I know it is, but sometimes you must face your fears.
You'll be happier if you can find ways to live with them.'

Mikah sniffles again.
'Are you coming with me?'

Mum smiles. 'You go first. I'll follow.'

Keeper Annie returns and Mikah leaps into her arms.
After a thumpity, bumpity ride through a maze of tunnels and trees,
they arrive at his new home.
Mikah sees huge green trees, big rocks and new swings.
It smells of pine and dirt, just like a jungle.

'Wow,' he signs.
'This is great.'
His new home is fabulous, but he misses his friends and his tree.

But what's that over by the big window?
Seeing a bunch of eyes gawking at him, Mikah grabs a vine.

He swings between the trees and lands with a thump.
It's them! His friends have found him!

The children press their faces against the glass.
Mikah does the same which makes them chuckle.

'You see?'
Mum is there.
'They came. It's okay to be afraid, love.
Just don't let it stop you from living.'
Mum beams, her eyes shining.

'Now look where we are living.'
She sweeps her hand around.

'Sometimes change is a good thing,'
Dad adds.

Mikah looks about...
The new house is bigger and better, he is safe with his family, and his friends are here.

But can he be happy somewhere new?
There is only one way to know. He needs to do the same things as always, test the idea...

So, the very next day-

He wakes up...
He eats breakfast...
He stretches...

He plays, struts and swings...

And although it's a different place, Mikah is fine. Nothing bad has happened and he even feels a tingle of excitement.

Some changes are good changes.
Mikah agrees this might be one of them.

Now to explore!

"What a joyful story for young kids. My daughter loved it and kept asking me about Mikah the day after. I would highly recommend this book."

Dr-Firas Al-Jabbari
(Located in Melbourne, Australia)

Printed in Australia
AUOW01n0153250618
299388AU00001B/1

9 780648 270409